Animal Craft Fun

Indoor and Outdoor Activities and Projects

by Beth Murray
illustrated by Ron LeHew

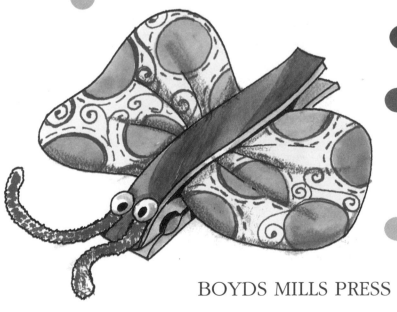

BOYDS MILLS PRESS

Published by Bell Books
Boyds Mills Press, Inc.
A Highlights Company
815 Church Street
Honesdale, Pennsylvania 18431
Printed in the United States of America

Publisher Cataloging-in-Publication Data
Murray, Beth.
    Animal fun : indoor and outdoor animal crafts and projects /
by Beth Murray ; illustrated by Ron LeHew.—1st ed.
[32]p. : col. ill. ; cm.
Summary: Crafts, recipes, and activities with an animal theme.
ISBN 1-56397-314-6
1. Handicraft—Juvenile literature. [1. Handicraft. 2. Games.]
I. LeHew, Ron, ill. II. Title.
741.5—dc20   1994   CIP
Library of Congress Catalog Card Number: 93-70873

First edition, 1994
Book designed by Charlie Cary
The text of this book is set in 12-point Century Schoolbook.
The illustrations are done in watercolor wash.
Distributed by St. Martin's Press

10 9 8 7 6 5 4 3 2 1

There's no place better to keep a letter than in a box half, fashioned as a giraffe.

Long-necked Letter Holder

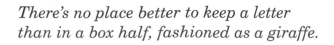

You will need:
- a cereal box
- yellow paint
- scissors
- brown paint
- a pencil
- a black marker

To make the Long-necked Letter Holder:

1. Spread newspaper over your work area.

2. Cut away the front, top, and side panels of the cereal box about halfway down.

3. Draw a giraffe head on the back panel of the box.

4. Cut around the head. Paint the entire box yellow. When the yellow paint has dried, paint brown spots on the giraffe and draw on a face with black marker.

5. Fill the box with cards and letters.

What's more fun than a barrelful of monkeys?
A long chain of chimps!

Chimp Chain

You will need:
- a long piece of paper
- a pencil
- scissors

To make the Chimp Chain:

1. Accordion-pleat a long piece of paper into folds about an inch across.

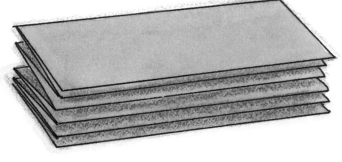

2. With a pencil, lightly sketch half of a chimp, being sure the center is on a fold and the hands extend to the end of the paper. That way the chimps will be holding hands.

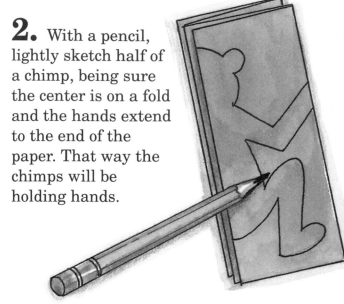

3. Cut out the chimps while the paper is still folded.

4. You can glue the Chimp Chain on construction paper to make a card. Or glue several chains together to make chimp streamers. Leave construction-paper chimps partially folded and your chimp chain should stand on its own.

Get in on the monkey business with this snack.

Monkey Bread

You will need:
- 1⅔ cups sugar
- ⅔ cup margarine
- ½ teaspoon nutmeg
- 2 teaspoons cinnamon
- 4 tubes of refrigerator biscuits (10 per package)
- a bundt or tube pan (a round baking pan with a hole in the center)
- vegetable oil
- a butter knife
- a large plastic bag
- measuring spoons
- a small saucepan
- a mixing spoon

To make Monkey Bread:

1. Wash your hands.

2. Ask a grown-up to help you preheat the oven to 350°. Grease a bundt or tube pan with vegetable oil.

3. Mix cinnamon and nutmeg with ⅔ cup sugar in a plastic bag.

4. Cut each biscuit into four pieces. Then put them in the sugar-and-spice bag and shake well. Place the coated biscuit pieces in the greased pan.

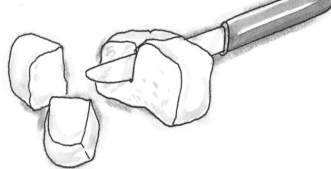

5. Have a grown-up help you melt the margarine in a saucepan over low heat. Add one cup sugar and bring the mixture to a boil, stirring constantly. Boil for one minute. Then pour the margarine mixture over the pan of biscuits.

6. Bake for 40 to 45 minutes. Ask a grown-up to immediately turn over the pan onto a serving plate.

See how many times you can make the crocodile catch the ball.

Crocodile Challenge

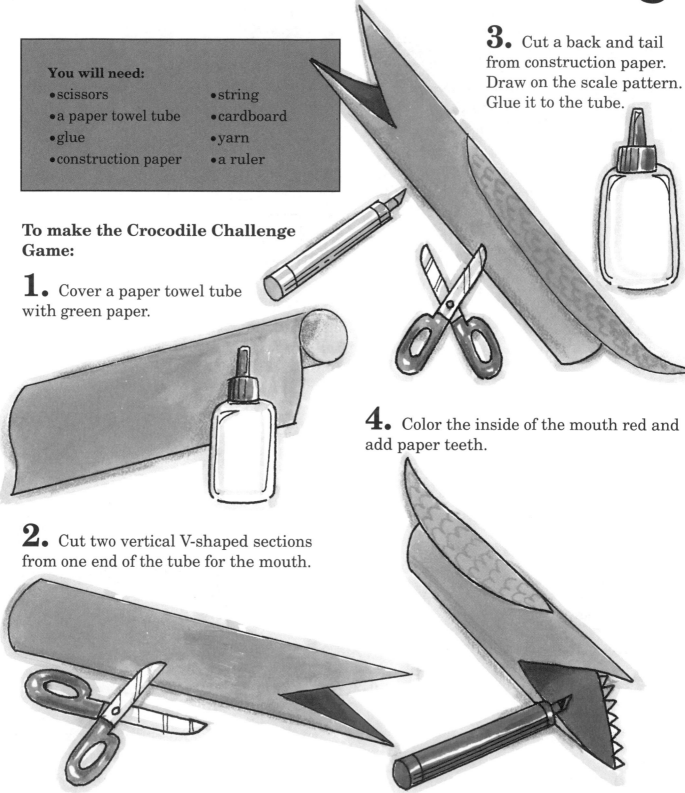

You will need:
- scissors
- a paper towel tube
- glue
- construction paper
- string
- cardboard
- yarn
- a ruler

To make the Crocodile Challenge Game:

1. Cover a paper towel tube with green paper.

2. Cut two vertical V-shaped sections from one end of the tube for the mouth.

3. Cut a back and tail from construction paper. Draw on the scale pattern. Glue it to the tube.

4. Color the inside of the mouth red and add paper teeth.

Game

5. Make a pompon by wrapping yarn about 30 times around a 3-inch cardboard square. Remove the yarn from the card. Tie an 18-inch piece of yarn tightly to the middle. Cut all the looped ends. Trim the pompon to resemble a ball. Make sure it's small enough to fit in the crocodile's mouth. Leave one end of the middle yarn about 10 inches long.

6. Poke a hole in the bottom of the crocodile's mouth. Slip the long yarn through the hole and tie a knot on the end of it, so it can't slip through the hole.

7. Toss the pompon and try to catch it in the crocodile's mouth.

Make your house a wildlife vacation station. These animals are looking for indoor vacation spots. Can you help any of them?

Vacation Station

Remember:
• *Have a grown-up make certain your guest is safe for keeping in your home.*
• *Wash your hands before and after handling your guest or its home.*
• *Be sure your guest always has clean water and fresh food.*
• *Set your guest free after a while. A vacation is not a vacation unless you return home at the end.*

Toad wishes to rent a terrarium with a broken-clay-pot room in which to hide. No sharp edges, please. Floor should be carpeted with crumpled leaves, except for damp, green peat (or sphagnum) moss in one corner and damp sand in another. Plenty of fresh water and a steady stream of worms, crickets, cockroaches, and small insects expected. A morning mist of water every other day would be appreciated. Call 555-RIBT for an appointment.

Grasshopper seeks a spacious gallon jar with air holes. Grass carpeting is a must. Be sure to have thick damp-sand padding below the carpet. Willing to share the jar with many small insects. Yum-yum! Jar owners, call 555-HOME. Insects, call 555-FOOD.

Box Turtle seeks a sunny, newspaper-lined aquarium with a clean, cereal-bowl indoor pool. Private shoebox room with cutout door would be very nice. Owner must arrange for regular exercise sessions on the lawn. This turtle also seeks a full-time cook who can serve earthworms, bread cubes, and mushrooms. The cook must make a good turtle salad with carrots, corn, peas, and kale. No lettuce allowed. Call after 5 P.M. at 555-SLOW.

Green Tree Frog wants to share a large gallon jar with crickets, flies, and moths . . . while they last. Air holes must not allow flies to escape. Floor may be damp moss or wet pebbles. No furniture necessary, but a plastic-plant staircase would be nice. Owner must lightly mist jar with water every other morning. Please write P.O. Box IMGRN, Stuckonatree, USA.

Jumping Spider seeks a gallon jar with air holes, plenty of sunlight, and a damp-sponge drinking fountain. Crumbled-leaf carpeting, several stick stairways, and a queen-sized central leaf required. Flies and other insects welcome as dinner guests. If interested, call 555-JUMP.

Camels live for days without food or water while their bodies use energy stored in their humps. Now you can get energy from a camel's hump, too.

Camel-Back Snack

You will need:
- an unshelled peanut
- a straight clothespin
- a brown pipe cleaner
- chocolate ice cream
- an ice-cream scoop
- a rubber band
- markers
- brown paper
- scissors
- a coffee mug
- tape

To make the Camel-Back Snack:

1. To make the camel's head and neck, attach a peanut to the top of the clothespin with a rubber band that circles around the middle of the peanut and between the two clothespin prongs.

2. Loop one end of a brown pipe cleaner into a camel-ear shape. Half an inch farther, make another loop. Attach the ears to the head by wrapping the rest of the pipe cleaner around the peanut. Draw eyes and nostrils with a marker.

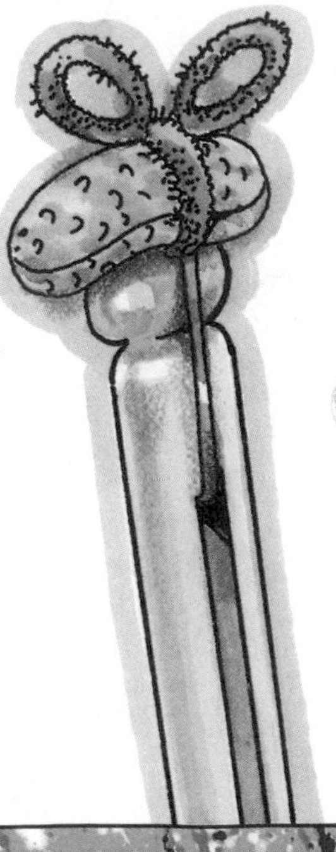

3. Cut a tail from brown paper. Attach it to the mug handle with tape or a brown pipe cleaner. Push the clothespin over the front edge of the mug.

4. Wash your hands. Fill the mug with a big scoop of chocolate ice cream to make an Arabian or one-humped camel. Use two scoops to make a Bactrian camel.

An elephant never forgets where you stopped reading.

Elephant Bookmark

You will need:
- an envelope
- scissors
- tape or glue
- markers or crayons

To make the Elephant Bookmark:

1. Draw the shape of an elephant's head at the corner of the envelope as shown. Cut it out, making sure not to cut the corner edges.

3. Color the elephant's head and trunk. Attach the trunk with glue or tape. Add eyes.

4. Slip the bookmark over the top corner of a book page to mark your place.

2. Cut a trunk from the leftover envelope.

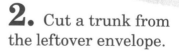

Fun is in the bag with this paper-sack puppet.

Brown-Bag Bear Puppet

You will need:
- a large brown paper bag
- scissors
- a pencil
- glue
- markers or crayons
- colored paper
- newspaper

To make the Brown-Bag Bear Puppet:

1. Cut down the side of a large brown paper bag. Then cut the bottom out of the bag so that you have a long flat sheet of brown paper.

2. Crumple the paper many times to soften it. Then flatten it out.

3. Fold the paper in half and draw a bear shape on it. Hold the paper together and cut out two bear shapes.

4. Glue the outside edges together, leaving the bottom open for your hand.

5. After the edges have dried, draw on eyes, a nose, and a mouth. Decorate it with colored paper.

6. Stuff crumpled newspaper into the head to add a little fullness.

Put your paper plates together and invite a dinosaur to dinner.

Prehistoric Paper Plates

You will need:
- six brass paper fasteners
- a paper punch
- paper plates
- paint, markers, or crayons
- scissors
- a pencil
- a stapler

To make Prehistoric Paper Plates:

1. Cut a head and a tail from a paper plate, as shown.

2. Cut two front and two hind legs from another plate.

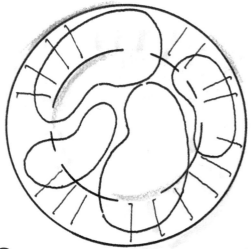

3. Punch a hole in each leg where it will attach to the body. Mark the points of attachment on two paper plates, which will make up the body. Poke a small pencil hole through each point (because the paper punch won't reach).

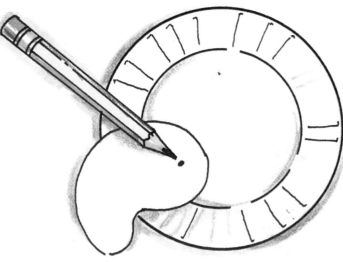

4. Attach a front and hind leg to each paper plate with four brass paper fasteners. Attach the head and tail to one paper plate with two brass fasteners.

5. Staple the edges of two paper-plate bodies together with the legs on the outside.

6. No one knows for certain the exact color or pattern of dinosaur skin. Use your imagination to paint or color your dinosaur as you think it looked.

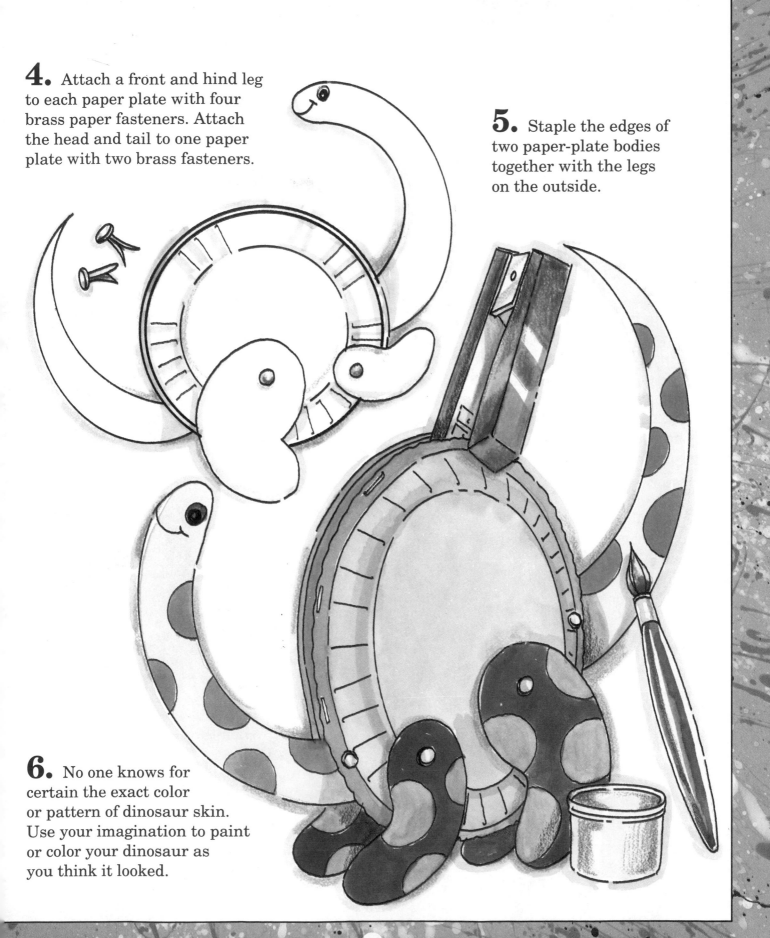

Bring out the beast in all your friends by throwing a Zoo Party.

Zoo Party

Here are some wild ideas to make sure everyone gets a lion's share of the fun.

Invitations

Fold a piece of yellow construction paper in half. Cut a banana shape through both layers. Make sure the banana will fit in your envelope. Glue the bananas together at one end. Cut a lengthwise slit in the top layer at the other end. Glue one of the cut sections down to look like a banana peel. Write "Go Bananas at a Zoo Party" on the peel section. Inside, write your name and where and when the party is to be held. You may want to color the ends brown or black to look like a banana.

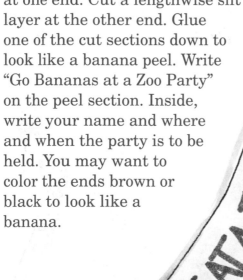

Decorations

Penguin Centerpiece

Wash and dry several uncooked eggs. Poke a small hole in the top and bottom of the eggshells. Hold each egg over a bowl and blow into one hole until the eggshell is empty. Cut a set of feet for each egg from cardboard as shown. Glue the eggshells

to the feet. When they have dried, paint the penguins. Glue a small plastic-foam ball to the top of each egg. Cut out orange beaks from construction paper and glue them to the heads. Decorate the heads with markers. Glue the penguins to a piece of cardboard covered with white paper. Glue cotton around their feet for snow.

Handy Hanging Octopus

Place your hand on a piece of colored paper with your thumb tucked under it and the fingers spread out a little. Draw around your hand with a pencil. Then do the same thing again. Cut out both hand shapes. Spread glue on the palm section of one cutout hand. Glue the two hands together without matching them exactly. Add eyes cut from paper. Finish the eyes and add a mouth with a crayon or marker. Punch a hole at the top of the octopus and attach a piece of yarn so you can hang it up. Make many of these and hang them all over the room. Or string them together to make octopus streamers.

Stick Zebra

Cover two empty cake-mix boxes with white paper. Add stripes with black tape or a marker. Cut holes in the boxes as shown in the picture. Glue the boxes together, matching up the holes. Add cut-paper eyes, nose, and ears. Glue on a black-and-white mane made of yarn or fringed paper. Push a broom handle through the holes. Put stripes on the broom with black tape. Add a rope bridle. Put Lena the zebra in a corner, though your guests may want to ride this decoration.

Games

Moose

Seat everyone in a circle. Let each player choose a different, easy-to-do animal hand signal like those shown. Go around the circle a few times with each person doing his or her signal, so the others can learn it. Then the moose starts the game. The moose does his or her signal followed by someone else's signal. The person whose signal came second then does his or her signal followed by someone else's, and so on. The object is to keep the signals following one after the other. See how fast you can go as a group. See how long the group can go without making mistakes.

Duck-Foot Relay

Make two pairs of giant duck feet. For each pair, cut two large duck feet from cardboard. Also cut two shallow tissue boxes in half the short way. Cover the feet and the box halves with orange paper. Glue a box half to each foot. To race, divide into two teams and set the turn-around point. One at a time, each team member puts on duck feet over his or her shoes and runs to the turn-around and back. The first team to finish wins. (The "trick" is to lift your knees high and move at a marching pace.)

MOOSE
ALLIGATOR
GIRAFFE
RABBIT
MONKEY
CAT

Food

Zoo Stew

Wash your hands. Combine 2 cups fish-shaped crackers, 2 cups animal crackers, 2 cups teddy-bear-shaped graham crackers, and 3 cups popped popcorn in a large bowl. Mix well.

Celery Snakes

Wash your hands. Wash celery and cut it into 4- or 5-inch pieces with a grown-up's help. Shape the snake's head by cutting a small triangle from each side about an inch from the top. Cut the two top corners of the head. Spread each piece of celery with cream cheese or peanut butter. Create snakeskin decorations with raisins, peanuts, olives, coconut, and bits of apple. You may want your guests to decorate their own snakes.

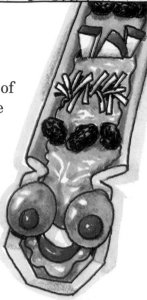

Party Favors

Elephant Nose

Cut twelve cup sections from an egg carton. Trim around the edges. Poke a hole in the bottom of each cup with a pencil. Make a knot at the end of a long pipe cleaner. Thread it through one cup section with the knot inside the cup. This will be the nose. For the trunk, thread on another cup but through the outside bottom of the cup. Continue with eight more sections. For the eleventh section, thread the cup through the inside like the first one. Then thread the last section through the outside bottom of the cup. Knot the pipe cleaner. Punch a hole in each side of the first cup section. Tie a piece of yarn to each hole. Place the trunk over your nose and tie the yarn behind your head.

Rumble Frog

Drop about twenty-five dried split peas, small stones, or pieces of uncooked macaroni into a green balloon. Blow up the balloon and tie a knot in the neck. Shake the balloon to hear it "rumble." On a piece of cardboard, draw large frog feet as shown in the diagram. When you cut the feet out, cut one slot in the front and one slot in the back, toward the middle. Then slip the neck of the

balloon into the back slot. Pull it forward under the feet and hook it in the front slot. Now the balloon will stand up. Cut out eyes from construction paper and glue them to the balloon. Draw a mouth with permanent marker. When you toss Rumble Frog into the air, it will always land on its feet.

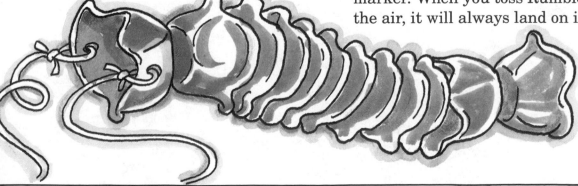

These are fish that come from tissue.
Try to make them, if you wish to.

Tissue Fish

You will need:
- colored tissue paper
- a small bowl or cup
- measuring spoons
- white poster board
- newspaper
- scissors
- water
- white glue
- a paintbrush

3. Brush an area of the white poster board with the glue mixture. Place one of the tissue designs on the glue area.

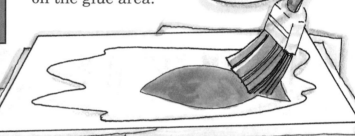

To make Tissue Fish:

1. Spread newspaper over your work area. Cut several fish and plant shapes from colored tissue paper.

4. Brush over it with more of the glue mixture, spreading some of the color to the white poster board.

5. Add more tissue cutouts to your picture. Brush over them with the glue mixture. Let the picture dry.

2. In a small bowl or cup, mix one tablespoon of water and one tablespoon of white glue.

There's something fishy going on.
See how many you can catch.

Go-Fish Game

You will need:
- construction paper
- glue
- scissors
- poster board
- a paper punch
- a dowel or stick
- string
- a paper clip
- a large, flat box lid or an upside-down shoe box (it should be at least an inch tall with a smooth surface)

To make the Go-Fish Game:

1. Cover the top of a box lid with blue construction paper. Cut several slits in the lid. Cut out waves from blue paper and glue them to the box-lid sides.

2. Make fish from poster board as shown. Punch a hole in the top of each fish. Stick fish in the slits.

3. Tie a piece of string to the stick or dowel to make a fishing pole. The hook is a bent paper clip.

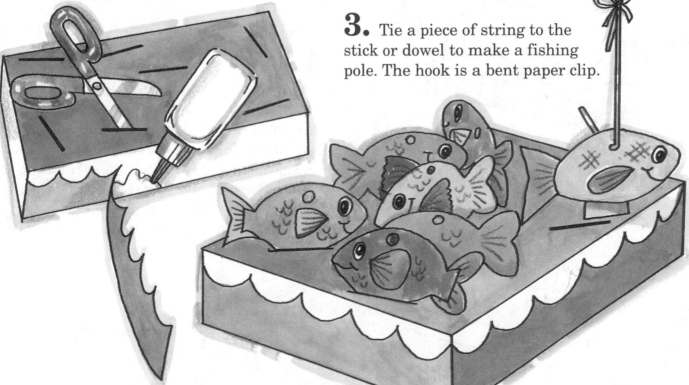

Invite a polar bear or an elephant to lunch,
you might be surprised by what they like to munch.

Beastly Feast

Polar bears like fish, and elephants like fruit. Don't you? Then get busy and fill your tummy with these beastly delights.

Polar Bear Pâté

Polar Bear Pâté
7-oz. tuna fish
6 T. mayonnaise
2 T. parsley
1 hard-boiled egg
salt and pepper
lettuce
an olive

You will need:
- a 7-ounce can of tuna fish
- 6 tablespoons mayonnaise
- 2 tablespoons parsley
- a mixing bowl
- salt and pepper
- a small saucepan
- a hard-boiled egg
- measuring spoons
- a mixing spoon
- a plate
- lettuce
- an olive

To make Polar Bear Pâté:

1. Wash your hands. Ask a grown-up to help you make the hard-boiled egg. Place the egg in a pan and pour in enough water to cover the egg. Bring the water to a slow boil, using low heat. Cover the pan and let the egg cook for seven minutes. Hold the pan under cold running water until the pan water is completely cold. Let the egg cool in the water. Peel and chop the egg in a bowl.

2. Add the tuna, mayonnaise, salt, and pepper to the egg. Mix well. Stir in the parsley.

3. Arrange lettuce leaves on a plate. Shape most of the tuna mixture into a ball. Flatten the tuna ball on top of the lettuce as the fish's body.

4. Make the tail with the remaining mixture. Add an olive for the eye. Serve with crackers and a spreading knife.

Elephant Apple Squares

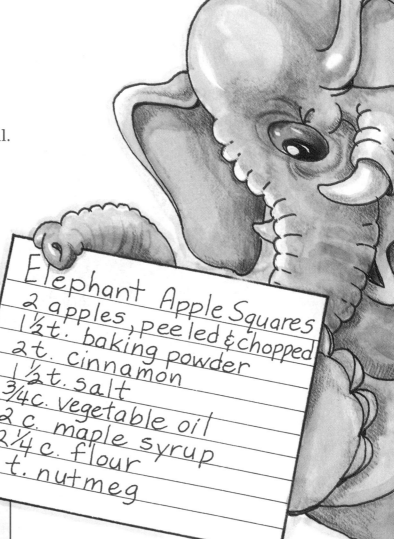

Elephant Apple Squares
2 apples, peeled & chopped
1½t. baking powder
2t. cinnamon
1½t. salt
3/4c. vegetable oil
2 c. maple syrup
2¼ c. flour
1 t. nutmeg

You will need:

- a 9-by-13-inch baking pan
- 2 apples, peeled and chopped
- 1½ teaspoons baking powder
- 2 teaspoons cinnamon
- 1½ teaspoons salt   • ½ cup raisins
- ¾ cup vegetable oil   • a butter knife
- 2 cups maple syrup   • a mixing spoon
- 2¼ cups flour   • measuring spoons
- 1 teaspoon nutmeg   • a large mixing bowl
- ½ cup applesauce   • measuring cups

To make Elephant Apple Squares:

1. Wash your hands. Grease the pan with vegetable oil. Ask a grown-up to preheat the oven to 325°.

2. In a large bowl, mix the flour, baking powder, salt, oil, applesauce, and 1⅔ cup of maple syrup (save ⅓ cup for the topping). Add the cinnamon and nutmeg. Then stir in the raisins and chopped apples.

3. Press the mixture into the greased pan. You may need to flour your hands to keep the dough from sticking while you flatten it.

4. Bake for 25 to 30 minutes. Drizzle the top with ⅓ cup of maple syrup. Let it cool, then cut into squares. Makes 24.

Invite animals and birds to visit with these treats and tips.

Backyard Buddies

Bird Feeder

You will need:
- scissors
- a paper punch
- a one-liter plastic beverage bottle
- sunflower seeds
- string
- a pencil
- a piece of paper

To make the Bird Feeder:

1. Wash the bottle and remove the label. Let the bottle dry. Save the screw-on cap.

2. Ask a grown-up to help you cut a tab about 1 inch wide on opposite sides of the bottom plastic section.

3. Bend down the tabs, and with a paper punch, make a hole in the center of each one. Push a pencil through the holes for a perch.

4. To make the feeding holes, press a crease along each side of the bottle directly above the two ends of the pencil perch. Holding the crease in place, punch a hole on the crease about 2 or 3 inches above the perch.

5. Roll a piece of paper into a cone shape and place it in the top of the bottle. Fill the bottle with seeds. Remove the paper and close the bottle with the cap.

6. Tie string around the lip of the bottle just below the cap. Knot it several times so that it will not slip off the bottle.

7. Tie the feeder to a small tree branch. Watch your feathered friends flock to it.

Goober is another word for peanut. Prepare this peanut pack and see who stops by for supper.

Goober-Grabber's Delight

You will need:
- an empty mesh vegetable bag
- twine or string
- unshelled peanuts
- scissors

To make the Goober-Grabber's Delight:

1. Put peanuts in the bag. Tie the bag tightly closed with string.

2. Cut two or three small holes on the top side of the bag, through which a peanut could fit.

3. Hang the bag from a tree branch.

4. Take note of which animals stop by to grab some goobers for dinner.

Welcome caterpillars and butterflies into your yard by planting some of their favorite foods.

Green-Thumb Greetings

Butterfly Buffet

marigold   aster
azalea   zinnia
goldenrod   lilac

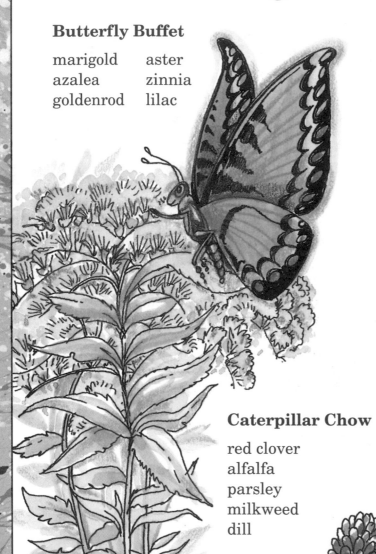

While waiting for the butterflies to discover your garden, make a butterfly of your own.

Butterfly Clip

You will need:
- scrap fabric
- string
- glue
- scissors
- a spring clothespin
- felt
- two pipe cleaners

Caterpillar Chow

red clover
alfalfa
parsley
milkweed
dill

To make the Butterfly Clip:

1. Cut a 3-by-4-inch piece of fabric. Trim the corners to make them round.

2. Tie a piece of string at the center of the fabric to gather it slightly as shown.

3. Glue this to the top of a spring clothespin, but leave a half inch of the clothespin showing at both ends.

4. For the body, glue a piece of felt on top of the fabric and clothespin.

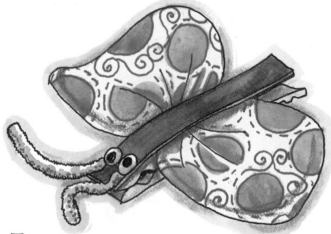

5. Glue on small pieces of pipe cleaner for the antennae. Add eyes.

6. Clip the butterfly to lots of things such as curtains, book bags, and planters. Or use it to hold notes and messages.

The Bird Word

Don't feed bread crumbs to birds. Plain bread is bird junk food. It fills their stomaches but gives them no nutrition. However, cakes made of bread crumbs and peanut butter are good for birds.

Make sure you have drainage holes in your feeder. Wet food gets moldy fast. Mold is poison to birds. So please clean your feeder often to prevent mold from growing.

If you want visitors, get a swimming pool. Many birds can't resist a cool, clean birdbath. You can make one easily using a shallow plastic container or dishpan. Cover the bottom with gravel and a few rocks, making deep and shallow places. Fill the container with water to 1 inch above the gravel in the deep end. Change the water every day.

Birds swallow little pieces of gravel and sand, called *grit,* to help them digest food. They usually find grit on the ground, but they appreciate bird feeders with dishes of grit attached.

Try these super cool treats.

Polar Pops

3. Put the cups in the freezer for three to four hours, or until frozen.

You will need:
- an eight-ounce container of flavored yogurt
- two ice-cream sticks
- two paper cups
- a spoon

To make Polar Pops:

1. Wash your hands.

2. Stir yogurt until it is blended and smooth. Spoon the yogurt into the paper cups. Place an ice-cream stick in each.

4. Peel off the cups and enjoy.

After you've licked the last Polar Pop, put your ice-cream sticks into a puzzling predicament.

Animal Puzzler

You will need:
- ten ice-cream sticks
- tape
- markers

To make the Animal Puzzler:

1. Wash and dry about ten ice-cream sticks. Line them up on a flat surface so they are touching each other.

2. Place a piece of tape securely across all the sticks. Number them in order.

3. Turn the sticks over and draw a picture on them.

4. Remove the tape and mix up the sticks.

5. Try to put your drawing back in order without looking at the numbers. You may want to share your puzzle with a pal. This is a great way to send secret messages.

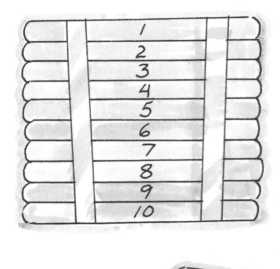

Dress your cat in its favorite coat print.

Cool Clothespin

2. Cut four leg shapes from the paper. Make sure they are long enough to cover the clothespins.

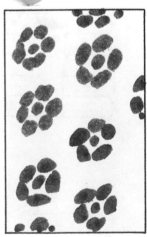

You will need:
- construction paper
- two spring-type clothespins
- glue
- scissors
- markers or paint

To make Cool Clothespin Cats:

1. Paint or draw the cat's fur pattern on construction paper.

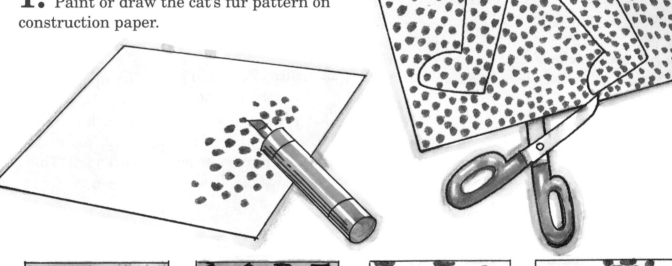

lion	tiger	cheetah	jaguar

Cats

3. Glue legs on each side of the two clothespins with feet at the open end.

4. Draw and cut the cat's head, body, and tail from paper. Add eyes, a mouth, and whiskers with markers or paint.

5. Clip clothespin legs to the cat's body. Position the legs so the cat will stand.

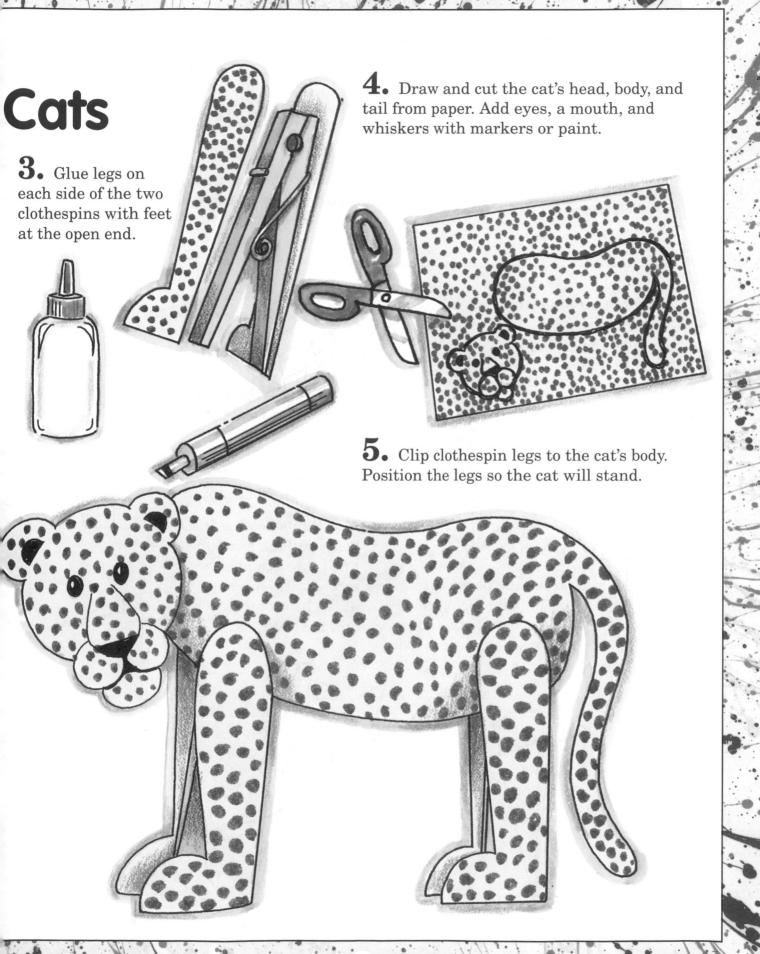

Begin with a square and end with a swan.

Origami Swan

You will need:
- paper

To make the Origami Swan:

1. Fold a paper square in half diagonally and crease. Unfold.

2. Set the paper with a creased point facing you. Fold the bottom two edges to the center crease to look like a kite.

3. Turn the paper over. Bring the folded edges to the center crease.

4. Fold the paper in half across the shorter middle width, with endpoints matching, to make a five-sided shape.

5. Fold the narrowest point down about 1 inch to form the head.

6. Fold the entire swan in half lengthwise along the center crease, with the head facing out.

7. While holding the body, pull the head up until the neck is straight. Crease paper at the base of the neck and the head.

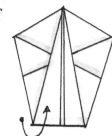

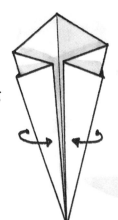